THE ENNEAGRAM PERSONALITY PORTRAITS

Enhancing Team Performance
Participant Workbook

Patrick J. Aspell, Ph.D.
Dee Dee Aspell, M.A.

ISBN: 0-7879-0888-6

Published by

An Imprint of Jossey-Bass Inc., Publishers
350 Sansome Street, Fifth Floor
San Francisco, California 94104-1342
(415) 433-1740; Fax (415) 433-0499
(800) 274-4434; Fax (800) 569-0443

Visit our website at: http://www.pfeiffer.com

Outside of the United States, Pfeiffer products can be purchased from the following Simon &
Schuster International Offices:

Prentice Hall Canada
PTR Division
1870 Birchmont Road
Scarborough, Ontario M1P 2J7
Canada
(800) 567-3800; Fax (800) 263-7733

Prentice Hall
Campus 400
Maylands Avenue
Hemel Hempstead
Hertfordshire HP2 7EZ
United Kingdom
44(0) 1442 881891; Fax 44(0) 1442 882288

Prentice Hall Professional
Locked Bag 531
Frenchs Forest PO NSW 2068
Australia
61 2 9907 5693; Fax 61 2 0095 7934

Prentice Hall/Pfeiffer
P.O. Box 1636
Randburg 2125
South Africa
27 11 781 0780; Fax 27 11 781 0781

Simon & Schuster (Asia) Pte Ltd.
317 Alexandra Road
#04-01 IKEA Building
Singapore 159965
Asia
65 476 4688; Fax 65 378 0370

ACKNOWLEDGMENTS

It is said that if we see farther than our ancestors, it is because we stand on the shoulders of those who preceded us. We too are indebted to the teachers and writers who have mined and discovered the hidden riches of the Enneagram: Gurdjieff, Ichazo, Naranjo, Beesing, Condon, Dobson and Hurley, Palmer, Riso, Rohr, and Wagner. All made original contributions to the development of the Enneagram.

Although we have milked many cows, the butter is our own. We have applied the Enneagram in many unique ways to business and organizations, as well as to education, psychology, and religion. Fortunately, we have been supported on our Enneagram journey by many friends. Our many thanks go out to the following:

- Marian Prokop, who was the prime mover of this Enneagram project and is the expert editor of our works;

- Maryann Morabito, who was an invaluable computer supporter;

- Jack Labanauskas and Andrea Isaacs, co-editors of the *Enneagram Monthly*, who published our many articles on the applications of the Enneagram to business, education, and counseling;

- Maurice and Tolina Doublet, Dee Dee's parents, who have encouraged us through the long years of Enneagram writing;

- David and Juanita Hammeren, our first printers, who believed in us and trusted in our dream;

- All the subjects who graciously consented to take The Enneagram Inventory® from its first version through its many drafts;

- Patrick, our son, whose patience and understanding allows us to devote long hours of labor to give birth to these materials; and

- God, who shared infinite gifts with us and brought our work to fruition.

CONTENTS

INTRODUCTION 1

What Is the Enneagram? 2

SELF-KNOWLEDGE AND KNOWLEDGE OF OTHER TEAM MEMBERS 3

Descriptions of Enneagram Personality Types 4

Personal Reflections 8

Team Analysis and Understanding 10

Notes 14

A PARTICIPATIVE LEADERSHIP/MANAGEMENT STYLE 15

Enneagram Leadership Styles 16

ONES: the Stabilizers 16

TWOS: the Supporters 16

THREES: the Motivators 17

FOURS: the Individualists 17

FIVES: the Systemizers 18

SIXES: the Teamsters 18

SEVENS: the Cheerleaders 19

EIGHTS: the Directors 19

NINES: the Reconcilers 20

COMMITMENT TO THE GOALS OF THE TEAM   23

Team Focus   25

RELATING EFFECTIVELY WITH OTHER TEAM MEMBERS   27

Interpersonal Styles   31

ONES: Perfecters   32

TWOS: Carers   33

THREES: Achievers   34

FOURS: Creators   35

FIVES: Observers   36

SIXES: Groupists   37

SEVENS: Cheerers   38

EIGHTS: Challengers   39

NINES: Accepters   40

Approach and Avoidance Behaviors   41

Notes   44

CREATIVE PRODUCTION OF RESULTS   45

Creative Team Problem Solving   51

Notes   54

TAKING ACTION   55

SELECTED BIBLIOGRAPHY   57

1

INTRODUCTION

Team empowerment consists of five elements:

1. Self-knowledge and knowledge of other team members;

2. A participative leadership/management style that encourages the sharing of individual talents;

3. Commitment to the goals of the team;

4. Relating effectively to others; and

5. Creative production of results.

The purpose of *The Enneagram Personality Portraits: Enhancing Team Performance Participant Workbook* is to enable you to find ways to work better with the other members of your team. This workbook is designed to build on the information that you learned as a result of your scores on *The Enneagram Personality Portraits Inventory and Profile®*.

However, some of you may be participating in these activities without having taken this inventory. If this is the case, be sure to read the descriptions of the personality types carefully and select the type that seems to suit you best. Remember, the descriptions are based on how a person of that type typically feels or behaves. You may find that you identify with more than one type; in that case, consider the one or two types that describe you best when you complete the activities that follow.

What Is the Enneagram?

The word Enneagram (pronounced "ANY-a-gram") is a combination of two Greek words: *ennea*, meaning "nine," and *grammos*, meaning "letters," or "points." The Enneagram system of nine personality types, in addition to describing each type, also charts the interactions among the various types. Therefore, the Enneagram offers a framework within which to appreciate individual differences.

In order to understand others, we need first to understand ourselves. Then, with this knowledge of ourselves, we can examine the ways in which we interact with others. In this workbook, you will examine interactions in two key dimensions:

- ▌ Center of Personality: Gut, Head, or Heart
- ▌ Teamwork Style: Adjustment, Cooperation, or Assertion

These dimensions offer important insights. By knowing, for example, which types are categorized as having a "Head" Center (FIVES, SIXES, and SEVENS), you can understand their focus on figuring out what is going on in a team. On the other hand, the teamwork style of a FIVE is "Adjustment," while the teamwork style of a SIX and a SEVEN is "Cooperation."

All of the activities in this workbook will help you and your fellow team members to work together more easily and more productively, with the good of the team taking priority over the individual preferences.

2

SELF-KNOWLEDGE AND KNOWLEDGE OF OTHER TEAM MEMBERS

Team planning and development requires knowledge. Knowledge of who you are—how you think, what motivates you, how you relate to others, and your work style—empowers you to plan your team and develop your interpersonal style. Knowledge of other team members empowers you with an appreciation of their individual frames of reference. Personalities can be understood in groups of three according to their centers, as shown in Figure 1.

Gut personalities (EIGHTS, NINES, ONES) tend to be concerned about their needs in a team, i.e., who they are and how they can take care of themselves. Heart personalities (TWOS, THREES, FOURS) wonder how they are doing with others and whether or not they are meeting others' needs. Head personalities (FIVES, SIXES, SEVENS) focus on figuring out what is going on in the team.

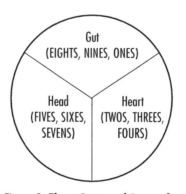

Figure 1. Three Centers of Personalities

DESCRIPTIONS OF ENNEAGRAM PERSONALITY TYPES

ONES

Perfecters like to excel in doing things well because they have high ideals. Uncomfortable with being criticized, they like to see themselves as good and right. Their strengths usually lie in the desire to be correct, conscientious, fair, and honest. However, they can be limited by the tendency to be critical, judgmental, and rigid. Their idealistic thinking is guided by objective standards and based on principles. They are motivated by the need to be right and to avoid criticism. In relationships, ONES are attracted to people who lead good lives and who value integrity and objectivity. They like to help others to improve themselves. Intimacy develops when ONES respond more to their feelings and needs than to "shoulds." They express affection in established ways at appropriate times and places. At work, ONES are generally task oriented, methodical, and hard working. Their personalities unfold as they strive for excellence and correctness. A ONE's sense of justice needs to be tempered by compassion.

TWOS

Carers are motivated by love to help others. They like to see themselves as giving and supportive. As good listeners, they tend to be empathic, friendly, and warm. However, because they are apt to be unaware of their own needs, they may find it difficult to say "no." Their affective thinking reasons from the heart or from their feelings and focuses on the concerns of others. TWOS are motivated by a need to care for and help others without being concerned about their own need to be nurtured. In relationships, TWOS are drawn to those in need, and they help in order to gain acceptance and affection. They can tend to flatter others for approval. Intimacy develops when TWOS let their own genuine needs be met by others. They are strongly committed to relationships in which they feel wanted. TWOS tend to be people oriented, altruistic, and generous in serving others. Their personalities unfold as they unselfishly fulfill the real needs of others. Their caring needs to be genuine in order to receive authentic love from others.

THREES

Achievers are motivated to succeed in reaching their goals efficiently. They like to think of themselves as worthwhile and desirable. Energetic and sociable, they are competitive and driven to attain results. Obsessed with social status, they may sacrifice relationships for career. Their enthusiasm and abilities to communicate make them effective in public relations. Their practical thinking puts ideas into action by calculating the means used for achieving results. They are motivated by a need to succeed and avoid failure. They are attracted to people with prestige and to relationships in which they can perform effectively. Assertive with people, THREES like to be close to others when they are doing something or engaged in social activities. Their personalities unfold as they are productive while being loyal to others. They need to balance success with integrity.

FOURS

Creators value introspection and sensitive awareness of their feelings and impulses. They see themselves as empathic and understanding. Desiring to be unique and genuine, FOURS like to express their feelings creatively in both serious and humorous ways. The depth of their emotional experience enables FOURS to appreciate art. They intuit others' feelings as they listen to them at work or at home. Their individualist thinking reasons according to what is meaningful to people and their feelings. In relationships, FOURS are drawn to people who appreciate them and withdraw in the face of misunderstanding. Intimacy develops as FOURS let go of the past hurts and find the good in other people. The personalities of FOURS unfold as they become fully aware of their unique personal goodness. Their sensitive feelings need to be balanced by rational thinking.

FIVES

Observers are attentive to data; they grasp and reflect on ideas and explain situations in the light of theories. FIVES think of themselves as knowledgeable and insightful. Their strengths lie in logical and objective reasoning, uncontrolled by emotions. Tending to be out of contact with their feelings, FIVES are not apt to become fully involved in the social world or to take action on their ideas. Their analytical thinking observes situations, reasons logically, and explains clearly. FIVES are motivated by the desire to know as much as they can and to avoid ignorance. Because FIVES tend to be emotionally detached in relationships, they are more comfortable sharing abstract ideas and thoughts than they are sharing personal feelings. In their work, they make good facilitators because they can summarize discussions and explain logically what is happening in groups. Their detached theoretical stance enables them to plan long-range projects. Their personalities emerge as they acknowledge the limitations of their own knowledge in the face of the wonders of the universe. Their thinking needs to be balanced by feeling.

SIXES

Groupists like to relate to people within a partnership, family, team, or community. Secure in their bonds with others, they are cooperative, loyal, and reliable. They think of themselves as dependable and faithful. They respect honor, tradition, duty, and obedience to the groups to which they belong. Their thinking is based on some form of authority, such as the leader, the group, tradition, or rules. They are motivated by the need to belong to a relationship and avoid disapproval and insecurity. Insecure feelings may lead to their being indecisive and over relying on authority. Once they are committed to a relationship, SIXES are faithful and give of themselves. However, they may find it difficult to receive from others. In their work, they are dedicated to a task or mission and collaborate with others. Their personalities are actualized as they face their fears and develop inner authority. Their fidelity needs to be directed more to the spirit of the law than to the letter of the law.

SEVENS

Cheerers are outgoing and spontaneous. Usually gifted with different skills and a variety of interests, they are enthusiastic in their enjoyment of life. They are optimistic as they look to the promising possibilities of the future. With a positive self-image, they are inclined to see themselves as happy. Usually on the go and fearful of pain, they may not appreciate the value of discomfort or suffering as challenges and opportunities for personal growth. Their positive thinking considers new and different possibilities and plans for future enjoyment. They are motivated by the need to be happy and avoid unpleasant experiences. In relationships, SEVENS are attracted to people who enjoy life. By focusing on the pleasing features of relationships, they manage problems and feel comfortable being close to other people. Ready to see the bright side of situations, they create a positive atmosphere for people to feel good at work. Their personalities emerge as they manage their impulses and deepen their appreciation of the meaning of suffering. Their anticipation of the future needs to be balanced by an appreciation of the present.

EIGHTS

Challengers are confident and easily assert themselves in deciding and taking action. They like to think of themselves as strong and powerful. They are fearless in grappling with problems and mobilizing people to get the job done. EIGHTS tend to regard gentleness as a weakness. Their type of thinking dictates opposing opinions and putting forth ideas forcefully. They are motivated by the need to be self-determining and to avoid submitting to others. Usually the dominant people in relationships, they feel capable being in charge. Intimacy develops when they are willing to be vulnerable in sharing their inner feelings. At work, EIGHTS make natural leaders and welcome difficult tasks, especially those that pertain to justice. Their personalities unfold as they come in contact with the tender side of their natures. They need to balance their caring for strength with the strength of caring.

NINES

Accepters are easy-going and stable. They get along with most people they meet. They see themselves as calm and accepting. Their patience, gentleness, and simplicity make other people feel comfortable and at ease with them. Their holistic thinking grasps similarities and plays down differences to unify different ideas into a harmonious whole. They are motivated by the need to live in unity and peace among conflicting parties. As NINES identify with people in relationships, they tend to feel close to them. Low in energy, they are not apt to control others. Their gifts of mediation enable them to harmonize differences within groups and make peace among conflicting parties. However, they may tend to gloss over problems and play down disagreements in order to avoid conflict. Their personalities are enhanced as they become more energized and enthused about developing their potential and confronting life's problems directly. Their desire for peace needs to be balanced by courage in facing the hard reality of conflicts.

Personal Reflections

Does the description of your personality type(s) fit you and how you usually experience yourself? Are the descriptive traits consistent with your personal experience of yourself? It is your decision to accept what fits how you see yourself. You can choose to reject whatever is inconsistent with your self-perception.

You may want to check the accuracy of your self-perception with the observations of someone in the team who knows you. You could invite that person to share his or her perceptions of you with you in an honest and gentle fashion. This person's agreement or disagreement with your self-perceptions can help you to discover your actual personality type. Self-discovery is a gradual, continual process of learning about yourself.

What do you think and feel about the type(s) that your reading of the descriptions of the types or your responses to *The Enneagram Personality Portraits Inventory and Profile*® showed you to be?

How comfortable or uncomfortable do you feel with what your profile reflects?

What is meaningful to you about your type?

What are the strengths of your type?

How could you use your knowledge of your type to benefit you and the team?

If you are not comfortable about your type, remember to keep in mind that no type is good or bad. Simply different types of people have different interests, talents, and styles of relating. Such different talents make each type unique.

In retrospect, remember that you are exploring preferences, meaning what you usually or actually like to do. Are you currently in a leadership or team position that does not fit your usual preferences? Or are you making changes? If you answered "yes" to either of these questions, you may be experiencing discomfort between what you actually like to do and what you are doing at present.

You may want to examine the desirability of your present situation in the team. Do you need to adjust to the situation in which you find yourself, or do you need to reassess your preferences?

Share your personality types with the others in your team. Remember that no one personality type is better than another. Each type is worthwhile in itself, including its strengths and limitations. The diversity of personal talents enriches a team.

TEAM ANALYSIS AND UNDERSTANDING

People interact with one another in teams in terms of similarities and differences. Although members of a team may feel most comfortable with people like themselves, they can be enriched by relating to people with different talents and gifts. In addition, a team usually requires different abilities for different functions.

The key to success is to integrate different personalities and different work styles into a cohesive whole so that the team can achieve its objectives efficiently. Otherwise, the differences are apt to result in recurring disagreements and conflict, thereby draining the team of its energy and subverting its effectiveness.

Instructions: Working together with your fellow team members, determine how many times each type occurs. Follow the instructions below:

1. Identify the team members who had one highest score, and list their names under the appropriate Enneagram types in Row A.

2. Identify the team members who had two highest scores, and list their names under the appropriate Enneagram types in Row B.

3. Identify the team members who had three or more highest scores, and list their names under the appropriate Enneagram types in Row C.

4. Total the columns by counting the number of names listed in each column. Write your answers in Row D.

Note: If you do not have results available for all team members on *The Enneagram Personality Portraits Inventory and Profile*®, use your knowledge of the Enneagram personality types to predict those people's types. Then proceed with steps 1–4.

TEAM PROFILE

Enneagram Personality Type	ONE	TWO	THREE	FOUR	FIVE	SIX	SEVEN	EIGHT	NINE
A									
B									
C									
D									

Team Profile

Use the information from the Team Profile to answer the following questions:

What types are most represented on the team?

What types are least represented on the team?

What difficulties might you personally have on the team with types that are least represented or not represented at all?

Do the types on your team complement one another?

What do you need to improve the effectiveness of your team?

Fully functioning human beings who strive toward peak personal empowerment recognize and respect differences in themselves and others. Furthermore, they have come to terms with the fact that differences do not necessarily mean "conflict." They have developed their responses to perceived differences to seize the opportunity to enhance their experiences of life.

Peak group-empowerment involves consistent support of others. Your experience as a member of a group or team can be empowering as you experience mutual invitations to stretch, grow, and get better at being the person you were created to be—for yourself and for the team.

NOTES

3

A Participative Leadership/
Management Style

One of the best ways to empower a team is to lead or manage with a participative style. Participative leadership expresses itself in different ways:

- Promoting effective communication among team members and with leaders;

- Expressing positions about problems and asking for input;

- Treating all employees fairly;

- Keeping an open mind that is receptive to other viewpoints and suggestions;

- Facing issues and inviting employees to cooperate for solutions; and

- Being attuned to workers' feelings and concerns.

Personal power is more effective than positional power for team leadership. Personal power is expressed through your personality type and leadership style. Different personal leadership styles enjoy different skills, abilities, experiences, and actions. Each leadership style can empower a team to work toward its goals.

Enneagram Leadership Styles

ONES, the Stabilizers

At their best, Stabilizers promote solidarity among employees by being sure that they conform to standards and work correctly according to established operating procedures. When disagreements arise, they refer to accepted policies that articulate the regulations to handle complaints. Preference is given to well-regulated organizations with clear cultural norms, such as detailed daily schedules and regular supervision meetings. Competency and skill at work are valued. Competent workers with the required technical knowledge are allowed to make decisions in their areas of expertise. As long as a team follows established policies, participative stabilizers are apt to give it responsibility for reviewing and assessing its progress on projects.

Performance, products, and services are expected to measure up to clear quality criteria. Precise, thorough directions are given to workers who are required to do their jobs well and complete them on time. Knowing how long projects take, they persevere to complete tasks. Workers are encouraged to be industrious, proceed methodically, and complete reports punctually. Motivated to live up to their ideals, ONES treat workers fairly according to the rules.

On the downside, if ONES become perfectionists, they rigidly follow standards and lack adaptability to a changing environment. As a result, they may lack flexibility in relating to team members. Fear of taking risks in ambiguous situations and concern about making mistakes inhibit innovation and creativity. Differences of viewpoints expressed by colleagues or members of the team may upset them easily and keep new, constructive ideas from emerging.

TWOS, the Supporters

At best, participative Supporters encourage team members in the development of their talents and skills by offering advice on how to do a good job and by praising them rather than using negative criticism. Training, counseling, and coaching are encouraged to help workers improve their talents. Their friendliness and cordiality make team members feel at ease in approaching them. As a result, workers tend to develop friendships and feel at home in the organization. Empathic with others' feelings, TWOS are concerned about the problems of workers, at times pitching in to help them complete tasks and being available to listen.

It is important to them how their decisions impact team members. Human resources and employee assistance programs are valued. Workers come to depend on TWOS and are encouraged to help one another. TWOS like to be liked and thanked by workers and recognized by their supervisors. The welfare of people is more a priority than the things to be done.

On the downside, over-solicitous TWOS may meddle in the personal lives of subordinates. If TWOS become codependent, they can let their own states of mind hinge on those of others, ignoring their own personal and professional needs. At their worst, they can manipulate team members with overly nice behavior, or workers may be controlled by flattery.

THREES, the Motivators

At best, participative Motivators inspire themselves and team members to perform and succeed by taking initiative, activating available resources, being efficient, and persisting to get results. THREES are effective communicators who greet and socialize with team members, remembering their names and faces. A winning impression is made by keeping a high profile with workers. Their enthusiasm stirs up workers' interests. Projects are pushed through quickly, even if it means confronting authority.

Workers are persuaded to achieve their goals and make the needed changes to get results. It is important for THREES to make progress in pursuing objectives until the desired outcomes are obtained. Ideas are quickly put into action and decisions are made rapidly to master tasks. Practical thinking empowers them to calculate useful means to their objectives. Competition among workers is encouraged to obtain fast results.

On the downside, to get immediate rewards, THREES may push through quick-fix solutions that cut corners and produce shoddy products or services. If their leadership becomes more style than substance, they may exploit workers and sacrifice human needs to advance their own career goals. As workaholics, they burn out themselves and their employees.

FOURS, the Individualists

At best, participative Individualists are interested in team members as individuals with unique talents. Sensitive to what is personally important to employees, FOURS give priority to feelings more than facts and are concerned about how decisions affect individual team members. The real feelings of people are intuited, and workers feel like they are heard and their feelings understood. The workplace is humanized with sensitivity and feeling.

Distinctly personal in their leadership styles, FOURS are original in imagining different ways of doing tasks and creating stylish products. Unique ways of accomplishing tasks are explored. Their new and interesting images enable them to explore alternative ways of solving problems. Creativity and imagination among workers are encouraged. FOURS excel as elite or charismatic authorities in charge of special projects. Recognition for having special skills in their fields is important to them.

At worst, moody FOURS may be unpredictable with employees, swinging between maximum and minimal expectations from team members. Sometimes they come across as over-concerned about people; yet other times, they are demanding. Their impractical and unrealistic solutions may lead to instinctive but rash decisions without basis in fact. Minor mishaps may be met with emotional overreaction.

FIVES, the Systematizers

At best, FIVES systematize ideas about tasks and situations to be sure they consistently fit into the organization as a whole. Participative Systematizers invite team members to share ideas about projects. Ideas are built into a vision to enlighten workers about the rational structure of the organization and show them its direction and purpose. Able to keep emotions under the control of intellect, Systematizers can plan long-range projects. Their decisions are based on well thought-out ideas that empower them to proceed logically in completing tasks.

It is important for FIVES to observe and gather sufficient relevant information to plan changes carefully, reflect and deliberate before making decisions, explore new strategies, and be certain before choosing courses of action. Analysis of complex issues into simple elements enables them to clarify the solutions to problems and understand what is happening in work situations. The reasons for any changes are explained clearly to team members.

Responsibility may be delegated to team members to enable them to do tasks in their own ways. Workers' responsibilities are clearly explained so that they can be certain about what is expected of them. FIVES prefer to set their own conditions at work.

On the downside, introverted FIVES may avoid face-to-face confrontation with subordinates, isolate themselves from colleagues, and not be readily available to employees. This style keeps them from bonding employees into a team. Communication is ineffective when they keep their expert knowledge and information to themselves rather than sharing with workers and when they fail to keep in touch with other leaders to implement plans of action.

SIXES, the Teamsters

At their best, participative SIXES think of themselves as part of a team with whose ideas they want to identify. Workers are encouraged to feel like members of a team and think about common goals. Members are encouraged to collaborate in setting objectives. Meetings are seen as group activities for promoting cooperation and friendship. Committed to the common good of the organization, SIXES place the team's well-being above an individual's interests. Loyalty, dependability, and hard work are valued to promote a team effort to solve problems.

Teamsters listen in a friendly way to workers; at times, they work beside them. Although SIXES prefer an alert and clear chain of command, group members may be given opportunities to help make decisions. Trust and collaboration are fostered among workers. SIXES themselves like a great deal of time to be sure of themselves before making decisions based on tradition and established practices. Workers are made aware of their duties and responsibilities.

On the downside, ideas and behaviors of subordinates may be controlled in the interest of conformity. Other leaders in the organization are approached with care, while those outside of it are regarded with caution or even suspicion. Unreliable or disloyal employees are ostracized or fired. New ideas and strategies may be met with defensive, secretive, and reactive behavior. Authority is exercised uneasily, with swings between self-doubts and bossiness.

SEVENS, the Cheerleaders

At best, participative Cheerleaders motivate team members to be enthused about their jobs. Although SEVENS dislike confrontation and enforcing decisions, they can interact with members who are different. Their optimism promotes a positive climate in a team and encourages members to anticipate positive outcomes to projects. Their inspiration to look on the bright side of challenging tasks boosts morale. A projected image of self-confidence makes them effective in professional situations. Easily adaptable to changing situations, SEVENS are attracted to different projects that excite their interests.

Team members are apt to be inspired by SEVENS' lively brainstorming of new concepts, creative solutions, and proposed changes. Their explorations of new ideas and promotion of alternative courses of action empower workers to learn innovative strategies and adapt to variable circumstances. It is important for SEVENS to place team members so that they enjoy their work and plan tasks in ways that guarantee satisfactory results. With speech enlivened by metaphors and stories, they persuade team members to adopt projects and take challenges.

On the downside, the reality of dealing with unpleasant issues may be avoided and decisions with unpleasant consequences may be delayed. Their dabbling in many projects without being attentive to details tends to prevent them from focusing on the completion of important tasks. Team members are apt to find themselves frustrated with the SEVENS' continually changing procedures. Impulsive commitments and vacillation in keeping agreements lessens their credibility with team members.

EIGHTS, the Directors

At best, participative Directors assert themselves in taking charge of challenging projects and rallying team members to get work done. EIGHTS make natural leaders who can stand up under the pressure of uncertain and turbulent business times. Prompt and tough decisions can be made independently of the team. Participative Directors have to make special efforts to let team members have input in decision making. EIGHTS are willing to take risks and even treat members roughly in order to complete projects. However, team members who are treated unfairly by others can be sure of the Directors' defense. Unproductive employees are readily confronted, and EIGHTS can persuade members to follow their ways of thinking.

Team members are persuaded in a firm manner to meet deadlines. Because Directors prefer jobs to be done their way, they work to eliminate resistance and obstacles. Disagreements are settled by command, and negotiations are carried out with aggressiveness and determination. Even in the face of strong opposition, they hold fast to their positions, quickly deciding to put ideas into action. Directors like to be kept up to date on information regarding changes.

On the downside, domineering EIGHTS come across as aggressive and intimidating. Orders are given in dictatorial or domineering manners. In their obsession to finish tasks, they can be insensitive to the personal problems and feelings of subordinates. Middle managers are apt to feel dominated by the strong wills of EIGHTS.

NINES, the Reconcilers

At best, participative Reconcilers harmonize the diversity among members into one team that can work together smoothly. Conflicts are mediated constructively and resolved as different sides of issues are heard, respected, balanced, and fused into an agreement that is acceptable to most, if not all. Their ability to identify with different viewpoints enables them to negotiate effectively. Team members are invited to make compromises for the sake of promoting peace. Tasks are assigned in clear and detailed language. Uncooperative or unproductive members are confronted in a smooth, nonthreatening manner. Patient and even tempered, NINES control their anger or displeasure with others.

Team members are empowered to get along together rather than compete, inasmuch as a harmonious team is apt to be more effective. Their holistic thinking concentrates on unifying different parts into a whole and synthesizing diverse viewpoints into acceptable agreements. Complaints are heard calmly and with patience to find agreement and promote consensus. Realistic and practical, NINES prefer to oversee routine, repetitive projects. With a preference for steady, stable changes, they take their time and deliberate before making decisions, especially ones that mean a change in the status quo. Set procedures are followed in solving problems.

On the downside, as a result of downplaying problems to accommodate others, NINES may procrastinate in confronting issues until they become critical. Petty details delay them from making important decisions. Innovative and challenging approaches that disrupt are not welcomed. Dissatisfaction is expressed in passive-aggressive behaviors, such as extended silences. NINES may not be receptive to critical feedback about their leadership.

As a participative leader, you are invited to complete the following statements:

I can promote shared responsibility on our team by...

I can ask for input regarding assignments by...

I can share information with team members by...

I can show how the particular contributions of team members fit into the
greater picture by...

I can encourage team members to share their knowledge and skills with one another by...

I can offer benefits for team performance by...

4

COMMITMENT TO THE GOALS
OF THE TEAM

The most important element of a team is its direction. Direction gives a team purpose, goals, and clear expectations. It is the team's reason for existing. Different team members focus on different aspects of goals and commit themselves by using their talents and abilities to realize goals.

Each personality type focuses on particular facets of the team as indicated in Figure 2. When leaders and team members experience congruence between their personalities and the team's needs, they are apt to feel comfortable and at ease at work. They experience the team's need for their contributions as well as their own need for the team. Feeling important, they find fulfillment in meeting goals.

PERSONALITY TYPES	TEAM FOCUS
ONE (Perfecter)	Correct order of tasks Quality performance of work
TWO (Carer)	Human needs Customer service
THREE (Achiever)	Results/outcomes Competition
FOUR (Creator)	Uniqueness of each person Distinctive product/service
FIVE (Observer)	Rational structure Critical thinking
SIX (Groupist)	Human relationships Commitment
SEVEN (Cheerer)	Satisfaction Innovation
EIGHT (Challenger)	Power/authority Action
NINE (Accepter)	Agreement and harmony Routine services

Figure 2. Enneagram Type and Team Focus

Team Focus

What is the purpose of our team?

How do I fit into the purpose of the team?

What contribution does the team make to the organization?

What specific, measurable goals do we have to reach the purpose of our team?

What results do we need to get to be sure that we are meeting our goals? Or what outcomes indicate that we are going in the right direction?

Commitment is also created by resources. More important than tools, materials, and money are personal resources. The talents and skills of each personality type and leadership style are the most valuable resources for meeting the expectations expressed in the team's direction. Sharing personal resources empowers a team with a sense of togetherness and belonging

Commitment develops when the leader and team members support one another by listening, celebrating, and recognizing. Active listening means attending to the words that are spoken, making eye contact, sensing feelings, and striving to understand. Celebrating can range from serving snacks to receiving special rewards. Recognition for work well done makes team members feel appreciated for their efforts.

5

RELATING EFFECTIVELY WITH OTHER TEAM MEMBERS

The morale and productivity of a team depends to a great extent on how well leaders and team members relate to one another. People like others to relate to them according to who they are and their individual personalities. Knowing how others want to be treated enables a person to treat them appropriately and encourages cooperation.

From your working knowledge of the Enneagram personality types, you can make educated estimates of the people with whom you interact. Summarize your understanding of Enneagram types by completing the sections that follow.

FEATURES OF ONES

FEATURES OF TWOS

FEATURES OF THREES

Features of Fours

Features of Fives

Features of Sixes

FEATURES OF SEVENS

FEATURES OF EIGHTS

FEATURES OF NINES

INTERPERSONAL STYLES

Different personality types have different interpersonal styles in teams, as illustrated below in Figure 3.

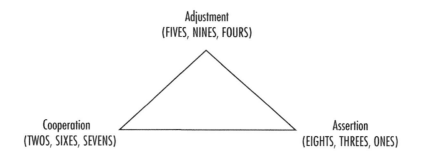

Figure 3. Interpersonal Styles

The Assertive types (EIGHTS, THREES, ONES) tend to move toward others in a team to take control of situations and strengthen their self-worth. Cooperative types (TWOS, SIXES, SEVENS) are apt to move with others to establish relationships that reinforce their personal worth. Adjustment types (FIVES, NINES, FOURS) are inclined to move away from other people to maintain their individual worth in a team.

On the pages that follow, you'll find suggestions of how to interact more effectively with people of the nine Enneagram types.

ONES: Perfecters

- Be honest and responsible.
- Respect established norms.
- Be punctual, stable, and conventional.
- Avoid being critical.
- Remember to keep agreements.
- Encourage them to improve performance.
- Emphasize the importance of rules and the right thing to do.
- Acknowledge them for having high expectations.
- Counsel them to correct their own mistakes.
- Praise them for working according to company standards.
- Be sure demands on their time are reasonable.
- Invite them to talk about feelings as well as "shoulds."
- Allow them to express their anger in safe ways.
- Express friendliness in accepted, customary ways.
- Show appreciation in formal language.
- Compliment them for being industrious and working hard.
- Acknowledge their quality performance.
- Be accurate in talking about the details of a project.
- Describe their roles clearly, according to accepted guidelines.
- Assure them of the right procedure in completing a task.

TWOS: Carers

- Communicate in a warm and friendly manner.
- Let them know their talents are needed in the workplace.
- Show acceptance and approval.
- Indicate that you are glad to be talking with them.
- Praise them for their caring and concern for others.
- Acknowledge them for their ability to be strongly committed to others.
- Affirm that it is fine to let others be in charge and make decisions.
- Praise them for giving advice and guidance.
- Commend them for serving others in need.
- Acknowledge their letting people depend on them.
- Notice their tendencies to flatter others.
- Affirm them for attending to the needs of people.
- Point out the importance of their being aware of their own needs.
- Acknowledge their tendency to neglect their own needs to please others.
- Compliment them for giving much of their time and energy to other people.
- Recognize their making coworkers feel welcome and comfortable in the organization.
- Be aware of their concerns about how decisions affect people.
- Thank them for being of assistance to others.
- Emphasize the importance of people over tasks.
- Make them feel cared for and at home in the organization.

THREES: Achievers

- Acknowledge them for being outgoing and sociable.
- Commend them for making friends easily.
- Compliment them for mixing well with people.
- Enjoy yourself with them at social activities.
- Provide opportunities for them to accomplish tasks.
- Challenge them to succeed at projects.
- Be effective in making your relationships with them work.
- Be aware that they may express feelings without inwardly experiencing them.
- Invite them to work at relationships as tasks to be achieved.
- Notice their tendency to put career before relationships.
- Be aware of their tendencies to impress others favorably.
- Engage in some activity with them to build relationship.
- Avoid expressing anger toward them.
- Communicate in an assertive, persuasive manner.
- Use time efficiently with them.
- Talk about the importance of getting results.
- Invite them to talk about how a job is going to be done.
- Praise them for efficiency in completing a task.
- Compliment them for working under pressure to get results.
- Be practical in talking about means useful for outcomes.

FOURS: Creators

- Recognize their tendencies to withdraw into themselves.
- Make them feel special.
- Commend them for wanting to feel self-actualized.
- Befriend by understanding them.
- Make being together a positive experience.
- Avoid miscommunication and misunderstanding.
- Assure them of the relationship, lest they withdraw.
- Give them the distance to stabilize a shaky relationship.
- Compliment them for the ability to see another through a crisis.
- Praise them for being able to handle intense emotions.
- Be attuned to their feelings of joy and sadness.
- Allow them to reminisce about the past.
- Help them feel secure enough to share feelings.
- Consult with them for useful information.
- Point out the uniqueness of relating to them.
- Invite them to express how they feel about a project.
- Acknowledge whatever special talents they have.
- Praise them for their imaginative approach to problems.
- Give them special recognition for their unique contributions.
- Speak in a personal way that is meaningful to them.

FIVES: Observers

- Take the initiative in talking and questioning.
- Share reflections on ideas about projects.
- Listen to their views and theories.
- Make observations about what is happening in a work situation.
- Avoid interpreting aloofness and detachment as lack of interest.
- Allow time for them to retreat from people to restore their energy.
- Avoid anger or intense emotions so they will not emotionally withdraw.
- Use thinking and facts rather than feelings in relating with them.
- Allow them time alone to reflect on issues before making decisions.
- Be ready to explain and analyze problems.
- Come across as intelligent, insightful, and factual.
- Communicate in a clear and rational manner.
- Analyze complex problems logically into simple issues.
- Theorize about the nature of projects.
- Prepare to answer hard questions by research and hard work.
- Assign projects for gathering data, systematizing ideas, and analyzing problems.
- Allow them adequate time to review and assimilate data.
- Set time limits to avoid open-ended analysis and discussion.
- Invite them to plan long-range projects with step-by-step procedures.
- Explore the broad theoretical underpinnings of their views.

GROUPISTS

SIXES: Groupists

- Emphasize the importance of loyalty and dependability.
- Build trust to attract their cooperation.
- Make them feel safe and secure in meetings.
- Compliment them for faithfulness to the organization.
- Come across as warm and friendly to gain their collaboration.
- Talk respectfully of traditions and duties in the workplace.
- Compliment them for supporting and accommodating others in the organization.
- Praise them for working hard and giving of time to others.
- Give clear guidelines and plans.
- Avoid giving confusing or double messages.
- Be sure their responsibilities are described clearly.
- Recognize their being punctual for work.
- Emphasize the importance of thinking for the common good of the organization.
- Allow them to feel secure within a circle of trustworthy people.
- Allow them to rely on authority for decisions.
- Talk through issues to help them feel better.
- Assure them of your reliability and concern.
- Speak and listen in a friendly manner.
- Be willing to defend and protect them.
- Emphasize the customary and established ways for working on a task.

SEVENS: Cheerers

- ▌ Be outgoing and friendly.

- ▌ Speak in a positive and optimistic manner.

- ▌ Validate their tendencies to laugh and enjoy work.

- ▌ Come across as a fun-loving person.

- ▌ Let them do many different activities or projects.

- ▌ Allow them to pursue their own interests.

- ▌ Acknowledge their attraction to a variety of exciting experiences at work.

- ▌ Be enjoyable company with them.

- ▌ Avoid confrontation.

- ▌ Commend them for encouraging others in difficult times.

- ▌ Present the bright side of work situations.

- ▌ Inquire about their pleasant experiences at work.

- ▌ Humor them and tell entertaining stories.

- ▌ Explore innovative strategies and new projects.

- ▌ Embellish your speech with lively and imaginative words.

- ▌ Talk enthusiastically about future plans.

- ▌ Avoid criticism and talking about routine work.

- ▌ Follow-up to be sure a task is completed.

- ▌ Check the quality of their product or service.

- ▌ Ask them about different alternatives for doing tasks.

EIGHTS: Challengers

- Relate in outgoing and sociable ways.
- Allow as much as possible their doing things in their own ways.
- Allow them to be in charge of projects.
- Be assertive and confident in relating.
- Talk in a direct and forceful manner.
- Remind them of social conventions.
- Praise them for being confident in making decisions.
- Be aware of their interests in having power or authority.
- Also them to present their views in strong and forceful matters.
- Gain their trust enough to let defenses down.
- Be fair in order to acquire respect.
- Respect their tendencies to protect and defend friends.
- Be ready for forcefulness in an argument, perhaps expressed with tough emotion such as anger.
- Be trustworthy in order to gain their confidence.
- Allow them to take action to complete tasks.
- Prepare to be challenged by their views.
- Compliment them for the ability to make tough decisions.
- Praise them for the courage to confront injustices.
- Inform them with adequate knowledge to make decisions.
- Recognize their independence and desire to be self-determining.

NINES: Accepters

■ Accept them without judging them.

■ Make them feel comfortable at work.

■ Accommodate their interests and needs as much as possible.

■ Acknowledge their readiness to comply with decisions of authority.

■ Listen to their views and opinions about projects.

■ Negotiate with them to come to agreement.

■ Compliment them for tolerating the opposing views of others.

■ Speak calmly and listen patiently to their complaints.

■ Harmonize differences in your relationships with them.

■ Keep in mind they tend to identify with your thoughts and feelings about yourself.

■ Allow them to be themselves while being friendly.

■ Talk about agreeable topics.

■ Be calm and relaxed when meeting them.

■ Relate in a way that has already been agreed on and accepted.

■ Commend them for working steadily and patiently at their appointed tasks.

■ Settle disagreements with them as soon as possible.

■ Allow them to do routine jobs and precise work with definite procedures.

■ Focus on facts and reason at a placid pace to a conclusion.

■ Avoid changing procedures frequently, or putting them in situations requiring a lot of energy.

■ Emphasize the similarities or commonalities.

APPROACH AND AVOIDANCE BEHAVIORS

When you relate to team members in ways they appreciate, they are apt to be trusting, cooperative, and comfortable with you. You are approaching others with positive behaviors, which in turn draws them to you—an approach situation. Figure 4 outlines ways to relate successfully to people of each type.

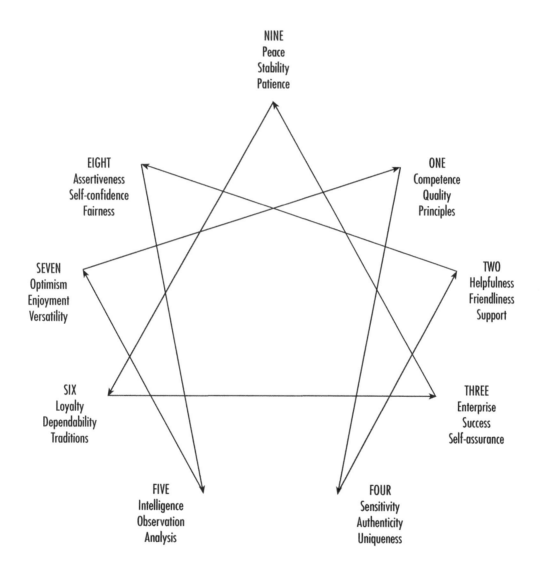

Figure 4. Approach Behaviors

In contrast, when you treat people in ways that they do not appreciate, you put yourself at odds with them. As a consequence, others feel uncomfortable, tense, and uncooperative—an avoidance situation. Figure 5 outlines behaviors to avoid when trying to relate successfully to people of each type.

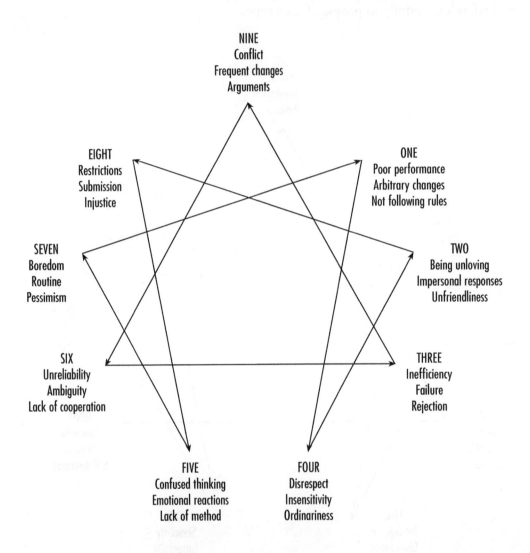

Figure 5. Avoidance Behaviors

Use the following outline to organize your thoughts about the likes and dislikes of each of the nine Enneagram types:

Type	Approach Behaviors	Avoidance Behaviors
ONE		
TWO		
THREE		
FOUR		
FIVE		
SIX		
SEVEN		
EIGHT		
NINE		

NOTES

6

CREATIVE PRODUCTION
OF RESULTS

A team produces results when it uses the talents of its members and their distinctive work styles. The use of these work styles at appropriate tasks empowers a team to be creative. It is important for the leader and team members to appreciate their individual work styles and utilize them to achieve results. The following pages outline the work styles of each of the nine Enneagram types.

ONES: Perfecters

▮ Work conscientiously to do a job correctly.

▮ Can stay at one task for a long period of time.

▮ Want to follow operational procedures.

▮ Dislike being interrupted at work by small talk.

▮ Want each particular step in a task to be done well.

▮ Like to be thorough and accurate with the details of a project.

▮ Proceed one step at a time in coming to conclusions.

▮ Want to be precise in stating facts.

▮ Think of ways to improve products and services.

▮ Want to treat people fairly.

TWOS: Carers

▮ Make people feel welcome in groups.

▮ Support people at work.

▮ Help others to do their work.

▮ Like to be with people in the workplace.

▮ Are interested in how projects affect people.

▮ Respond to the needs of others.

▮ Focus on how people are affected by decisions.

▮ Like to be thanked.

▮ Tend to be sympathetic to peoples' needs.

▮ Show people that they are interested in them.

THREES: Achievers

- Motivate others to do their jobs.
- Enjoy talking with others about tasks.
- Work efficiently to get results.
- Communicate by talking about accomplishments.
- Can recall people's names.
- Want results as soon as possible.
- Can work under pressure to get things done quickly.
- Usually pursue goals until they reach them.
- Decide practical ways to use resources.
- Talk with enthusiasm to persuade people.

FOURS: Creators

- Are concerned about people's feelings.
- Sound out their feelings before acting.
- Prefer inner communication with their own feelings and emotions.
- Like to come in contact with how they feel about projects.
- Can be imaginative in exploring new possibilities.
- Tend to imagine unique ways to get work done.
- Dislike doing the same ordinary work repeatedly.
- Enjoy acquiring special skills for dealing with unique situations.
- May alternate between enthusiasm and lessening of interest in projects.
- May be artistic or aesthetic in their approaches to situations.

FIVES: Observers

▮ Are good at analyzing problems.

▮ Reflect on the theories behind projects.

▮ Are satisfied working by themselves.

▮ Prefer silence in order to concentrate.

▮ Dislike being interrupted by phone calls on the job.

▮ Reflect for a time before taking action, sometimes neglecting to act.

▮ Can apply themselves to tasks for long periods of time.

▮ Like to learn about projects by listening to tapes or reading alone.

▮ Explore the speculative possibilities of theories and ideas.

▮ Like acquiring new insights and thinking skills.

SIXES: Groupists

▮ Are cooperative with people in their groups.

▮ Like to work with reliable people.

▮ Can work hard and continually on one task without breaks.

▮ Feel secure working within groups or organizations.

▮ Favor communication within a circle of trustworthy people.

▮ Like to relate to people who belong to their groups or organizations.

▮ Like the customary and established ways of working.

▮ Keep traditions and duties in mind while carefully coming to decisions.

▮ Want to be sure how groups see the facts.

▮ Get to work on time.

SEVENS: Cheerers

- Enjoy a variety of interests.
- Tend to be impatient with routine jobs.
- Like talking with people.
- Usually move quickly, sometimes impulsively.
- Like to familiarize themselves with new projects by talking with others.
- Want to enjoy their work.
- Are interested in innovative ideas and the possibilities of situations.
- May become involved in more than one project.
- Get enthused easily about new projects.
- Like making people happy.

EIGHTS: Challengers

- Like to take action.
- Are interested in taking charge of projects.
- Can be tough minded and direct.
- Can rebuke or reprimand others when necessary.
- Can make quick decisions.
- Like to complete the projects they start.
- Are willing to take on challenging projects.
- Can rally people to meet deadlines.
- Can work under pressure to get a job done.
- Want to convince people to do things their way.

NINES: Accepters

- Make people feel at ease.
- Like people to get along at work.
- Are concerned about people working in harmony.
- Want to be calm and collected during every step of a task.
- Like to follow agreements that already have been accepted by others.
- Like disagreements to be settled as soon as possible.
- Reason calmly one step at a time until they reach conclusions.
- Consider the facts patiently.
- Like to accommodate people.
- Get along with different kinds of people.

CREATIVE TEAM PROBLEM SOLVING

Results can be produced more creatively by team problem solving. Identifying individual styles of problem solving empowers the team to use the special talents of each member more creatively. In this way, each style contributes to the overall effort of teamwork and improves its effectiveness in accomplishing tasks.

As illustrated in Figure 6, progress in problem solving requires a forward movement of the mind. The process begins with the relevant facts and data that describe the problem, moves to possible solutions, proceeds to an understanding of the meaning of the consequences, and goes on to an appreciation of the impacts on people, and finally to the attainment of results, which can become data for further problem solving.

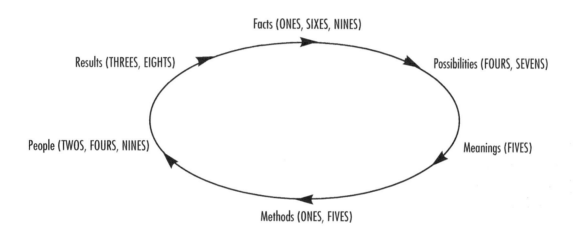

Figure 6. Model of Enneagram Problem Solving

Various Enneagram types focus differently on problem solving. Consider the following examples:

- ONES, SIXES, and NINES focus on facts.

- FOURS and SEVENS consider possibilities.

- FIVES concentrate on meanings.

- ONES and FIVES focus on methods.

- TWOS, FOURS, and NINES attend to people.

- THREES and EIGHTS center on results.

The next figure (Figure 7) shows the problem-solving style of the various Enneagram types in another way.

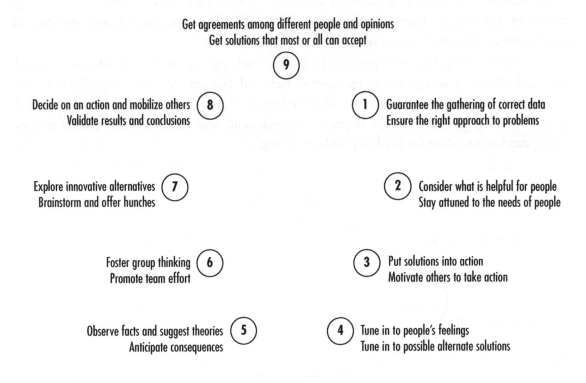

Get agreements among different people and opinions
Get solutions that most or all can accept
9

Decide on an action and mobilize others 8
Validate results and conclusions

1 Guarantee the gathering of correct data
Ensure the right approach to problems

Explore innovative alternatives 7
Brainstorm and offer hunches

2 Consider what is helpful for people
Stay attuned to the needs of people

Foster group thinking 6
Promote team effort

3 Put solutions into action
Motivate others to take action

Observe facts and suggest theories 5
Anticipate consequences

4 Tune in to people's feelings
Tune in to possible alternate solutions

Figure 7. Personal Creative Problem Solving

Consider the following questions:

What are your talents or strengths as a team in problem solving?

What are your blind spots or limitations as a team?

How could your team be more effective in problem solving?

NOTES

7

TAKING ACTION

Knowledge, to be useful, needs to be put into action. This last activity is to help you complete the journey with "a bang and not a whimper" (apologies to T.S. Eliot).

The fully functioning human being actualizes peak self-empowerment by consistently applying insights and skills to his or her life. Please complete the following statements:

1. We learned that our team is...

2. We realize that our team has talents or strengths such as...

3. We know that we can develop ourselves as a team by...

4. We have decided to put the following ideas into action:

a.

b.

c.

5. We will take action on these things by doing these specific behaviors:

a.

b.

c.

6. We will check our progress at least once a week by observing, reflecting, and completing the following statements:

a. We see a difference in ourselves because…

b. We experience a difference in our team because…

c. We grasp a difference in our behavior at work because…

d. We sense a difference in the work world around us because…

You are invited to share your responses with team members. Remember: Actions speak louder than words.

8

SELECTED BIBLIOGRAPHY

Aspell, D.D., & Aspell, P.J. (1990). *Chart of the Enneagram Personality Types*. San Antonio, TX: Lifewings® Ltd.

Aspell, D.D., & Aspell, P.J. (1991). *Profiles of the Enneagram: Ways of Coming Home to Yourself.* San Antonio, TX: Lifewings® Ltd.

Aspell, D.D., & Aspell, P.J. (1992). *Unlimited Empowerment: Discovering and Enhancing Your Personal Professional Life via the Enneagram*. San Antonio, TX: Lifewings® Ltd.

Aspell, D.D., & Aspell, P.J. (1993). *Empowering Relationships: Discovering and Enhancing Your Personal and Interpersonal Life via the Enneagram*. San Antonio, TX: Lifewings® Ltd.

Aspell, D.D., & Aspell, P.J. (1994). *Building Better Relationships with People*. San Antonio, TX: Lifewings® Ltd.

Aspell, D.D., & Aspell, P.J. (1994). *Career and Life Management*. San Antonio, TX: Lifewings® Ltd.

Aspell, D.D., & Aspell, P.J. (1994). *Chart of the Nine Enneagram Personality Types and Professional Styles*. San Antonio, TX: Lifewings® Ltd.

Aspell, D.D., & Aspell, P.J. (1994). *Creating Teams and Building Teamwork*. San Antonio, TX: Lifewings® Ltd.

Aspell, D.D., & Aspell, P.J. (1994). *The Discovery and Development of Effective Personal Leadership*. San Antonio, TX: Lifewings® Ltd.

Aspell, D.D., & Aspell, P.J. (1994). *Profiles of the Nine Personal Professional Enneagram Styles*. San Antonio, TX: Lifewings® Ltd.

Aspell, D.D., & Aspell, P.J. (1995). *Discovering Yourself and Developing Your Style of Leadership, Supervision, and Counseling*. San Antonio, TX: Lifewings® Ltd.

Aspell, D.D., & Aspell, P.J. (1995). *Enneagram Communication Styles*. San Antonio, TX: Lifewings® Ltd.

Aspell, D.D., & Aspell, P.J. (1995). *Enneagram Learning Styles*. San Antonio, TX: Lifewings® Ltd.

Aspell, D.D., & Aspell, P.J. (1995). *Enneagram Teaching and Training Styles*. San Antonio, TX: Lifewings® Ltd.

Aspell, D.D., & Aspell, P.J. (1995). *Enneagram Thinking and Problem Solving Styles*. San Antonio, TX: Lifewings® Ltd.

Aspell, D.D., & Aspell, P.J. (1995). *Enneagram Transparencies*. San Antonio, TX: Lifewings® Ltd.

Aspell, D.D., & Aspell, P.J. (1995). *How to Use the Enneagram for Effective Counseling*. San Antonio, TX: Lifewings® Ltd.

Aspell, D.D., & Aspell, P.J. (1995). Leadership Styles and the Enneagram, in J.W. Pfeiffer (Ed.), *The 1995 Annual: Volume 1, Training* (pp. 227-241). San Francisco: Pfeiffer, An Imprint of Jossey-Bass Inc., Publishers.

Aspell, D.D., & Aspell, P.J. (1995). *Letting Go of Irritants*. San Antonio, TX: Lifewings® Ltd.

Aspell, D.D., & Aspell, P.J. (1995). *Managing Conflict the Enneagram Way*. San Antonio, TX: Lifewings® Ltd.

Aspell, D.D., & Aspell, P.J. (1995). *Using the Enneagram to Empower Organizations*. San Antonio, TX: Lifewings® Ltd.

Aspell, D.D., & Aspell, P.J. (1995). *Using the Enneagram to Build Better Marital Relationships*. San Antonio, TX: Lifewings® Ltd.

Aspell, D.D., & Aspell, P.J. (1996). *The Eloquent Enneagrammer: Quality Presentation and Speaking*. San Antonio, TX: Lifewings® Ltd.

Aspell, D.D., & Aspell, P.J. (1996). *The Enterprising Enneagrammer: How to Use the Enneagram to Generate Sales*. San Antonio, TX: Lifewings® Ltd.

Aspell, D.D., & Aspell, P.J. (1996). *Journey from Type to Archetype: Jungian Personality Type Inventory and Archetype Inventory* . San Antonio, TX: Lifewings® Ltd.

Aspell, D.D., & Aspell, P.J. (1996). *The Jungian Personality Type Inventory* . San Antonio, TX: Lifewings® Ltd.

Aspell, D.D., & Aspell, P.J. (1996). *The Lawyer's Enneagram*. San Antonio, TX: Lifewings® Ltd.

Aspell, D.D., & Aspell, P.J. (1996). *The Nine Enneagram Negotiation Styles*. San Antonio, TX: Lifewings® Ltd.

Aspell, D.D., & Aspell, P.J. (1996). *Portraits of Enneagram Relationships: Nine Relational and Forty-Five Interpersonal Enneagram Relationships*. San Antonio, TX: Lifewings® Ltd.

Covey, S.R. (1990). *The Seven Habits of Highly Effective People*. New York: Simon & Schuster.

Covey, S.R. (1991). *Principle-Centered Leadership*. New York: Simon & Schuster.

Forster, S., & O'Hanrahan, R. (1994). *Understanding Personality Types in the Workplace*. Oakland, CA: Authors.

Palmer, H. (1995). *The Enneagram in Love and Work*. San Francisco: HarperCollins.

Printed and bound by CPI Group (UK) Ltd, Croydon, CR0 4YY

09/06/2025

14685917-0003